THE DECLINE AND FALL OF THE ROMAN EMPIRE

THE DECLINE AND FALL OF THE ROMAN EMPIRE

Matthew Tuckner

Four Way Books
Tribeca

Library of Congress Cataloging-in-Publication Data

Names: Tuckner, Matthew author
Title: The decline and fall of the Roman Empire / Matthew Tuckner.
Other titles: Decline and fall of the Roman Empire (Compilation)
Description: Tribeca : Four Way Books, 2025.
Identifiers: LCCN 2025003858 (print) | LCCN 2025003859 (ebook) | ISBN 9781961897540 trade paperback | ISBN 9781961897557 ebook
Subjects: LCGFT: Poetry
Classification: LCC PS3620.U337 D43 2025 (print) | LCC PS3620.U337 (ebook) | DDC 811/.6--dc23/eng/20250206
LC record available at https://lccn.loc.gov/2025003858
LC ebook record available at https://lccn.loc.gov/2025003859

This book is manufactured in the United States of America and printed on acid-free paper.

Four Way Books is a not-for-profit literary press. We are grateful for the assistance we receive from individual donors, public arts agencies, and private foundations including the New York State Council on the Arts, a state agency.

We are a proud member of the Community of Literary Magazines and Presses.

Contents

for M.C.R

What holds me here destroys me as I go.

—Jane Mead

The Decline and Fall of the Roman Empire

The Getty

Because I am one of time's children,
things happen to me.

Tourists pick the poblanos
from their burritos to feed the seabirds.

Planes drop clouds of red phosphorus
on the ashy birches.

A man in a Tom Brady jersey
nearly stumbles into the bust

of an emperor who
slaughtered his own brother.

The sky looks wrong. My spit is brown.
I won't be here for very long.

Van Gogh's *Irises* keep humming
from the walls, knowing

they'll outlive me,

that the violet paint they don

oozes a stillness that will be
still forever. It's simple really.

I might just close my eyes
& do it, a friend told me

two days before she just
closed her eyes & did it.

There are so many people no longer
happening, it almost makes a sound.

I.

The Decline and Fall of the Roman Empire

A city unfurls like a sneeze
          across the hillside.
The present tense blurs.
          The viaduct sprouts more viaduct.
The water tastes like prune juice
          & there are endless reserves of it.
Thinking is the mind's problem,
          the philosophers write, so thinking stops,
despite the raindrops
          dotting the slip n' slide
in ungodly patterns,
          despite the oracle's efforts to trace
the strange shapes into perfect umlauts
          of destiny, to no avail.
Over a dinner of boiled flamingo,
          a father promises his son he will live forever.
Tomorrow, he will be shot
          while conjugating verbs on the blackboard.
Tomorrow, it will be today again,
          whole lives tucked between
the words *is* & *was*.
          A box of swifts is flying headfirst
into a cloud of methane.
          A cherry popsicle is time-lapsing

into liquid in the tall grass.
            A general, believing his enemies
are hidden beneath the wine-dark waves,
            is forcing his soldiers to march,
one by one, into the sea.

The Decline and Fall of the Roman Empire

Near the end of his life, the artist painted six coffins
egg-shell white, filling them with the cadavers

of diseased sea stars found in tidepools
along the coast of San Luis Obispo.

When we enter the gallery, you spill the contents
of your tote bag into a metal tray: camera lens, pill organizer,

a fragment of orange rind shaped like Florida,
a bottle of smartwater, dyed gold with powdered electrolytes.

Only one canvas grabs your fleeting attention: abstract clots
of cloud, swirling with menace above a baby in a bassinet.

We know what's coming. We've been texting back & forth
famous last words as a way of making light of it,

a record of the mind speaking to the mind in dulcet tones,
reminding the mind it remains here for now.

Heraclitus: *Can you turn wet water into dry?*
Caligula: *I am still very much alive.*

It appears that what will happen hasn't
happened yet. So we fill the time with projects,

Tokyo, memories of its greedy koi fish, a ceramic bowl
of goji berries perfectly balanced on a tree branch.

We fatten the time until it bursts into artifacts:
sixteen photographs of a single puddle

taking shape in the red glow of your darkroom.
A puddle you glimpsed the moon in & stopped for.

A puddle that was just plain rain until it fell.

The Decline and Fall of the Roman Empire

There's a menace to how the big-eyed robot
in Stop & Shop swivels its neck to scour for shoplifters
that makes me feel like I've skirted the highway
from past to future in less than a minute,
pit-stopping along the way to flatten a few specimens
between the pages of my books, each California poppy
autotuned to twin the orange of its neighbor,
each tire-blown tidy tip easily mistaken for a cupcake liner.
There are rats in there, my partner says, pointing at the aperture
splitting the biggest oak in our park,
just missing the flurry of a tail before it disappears
beneath the aegis of an Amazon box.
Earlier, we woke up, slapped some blood into our toes,
ruined perfect mugs of water with whatever
the Folgers can would offer & did our part
to deworm the kittens that roam our apartment.
Argyle hissed, but Jelly Bean relented, rubbing the rumored
pheromones of her chin against the curve of my knuckle,
freckling against my chest so gently I tried to stay
as still as a mother. It's an honor, to wander the avenues
of the city with the scent of her happiness on my fist,
to swan dive over a crow draining the pulse from what's left
of a pigeon, to pluck the ivory harp of everything
so monstrously loud, I almost forget how all of it is out to get us.

How, for a friend, each paddle smacking the East River
is her father's hand, each chaste blueberry we pull
from the earth for our crumble the early mauve of a bruise.
How my grandfather, who can no longer tell you
what planet he's on, murmurs the name
of his savior, drops to his knees in the snack aisle,
& begs the robot for his mind back.

The Decline and Fall of the Roman Empire

The pianist rubs the misery from his face
with the heel of his hand & counts
the trio into an original that sounds
like it misses its mother.
You are not in my head with me.
There's only a half milligram of Ativan.
A few conditional clauses about the weather
& the varied textures of foreign coins.
When you are well, we text about seed vaults,
the shelf life of Twinkies, how you still haven't given
the tumor digging into your back a name.
It's enough to make you cry,
how each moment is choked up
with so much writhing potential
that the notion of *moment* fades away,
the dreams bleeding directly into life.
Last night: the recurring image of a school
of carp congealed on the wings
of a black swan like shirtsleeves,
begging the bird for its food.
The pianist segues into a new number,
something modal & sad called *Hunchback*.
I am not in your body with you.
Today, I ate a white chocolate bunny

suffused with cannabis, & thought
of the dusty red carpet
in the John Keats house, the headless
mannequins wearing his suits.
Using my eyes, I went & looked at art so barely
even there that it seemed to have everything
to say about nothingness.
Piles of chalk spilled across
four giant mirrors on the floor.
An almost-blank canvas the painter titled
I Love the Whole World.

The Decline and Fall of the Roman Empire

The therapist asks me to move my eyes from left to right
    & describe what my body feels like.

A cream-filled profiterole. The itchy bites
    the no-see-ums pepper along a shoulder blade.

C. says that the surgery on his lung will take a matter
    of minutes, but to remove the masses

from his abdomen is an entirely different animal.
    He is 60% water. He has the word *mom*

tattooed on the inside of his finger.
    In a lecture, Derrida deconstructed Heidegger,

claiming that the metaphors for *being* are never stable.
    My sister, who smokes pot from a pipe blown

in the shape of a frog, texts me a picture of a glasswing
    butterfly gone pink against a lantana flower.

Between hits, she will often ask, *who am I?*
    Yesterday it was taxes, a book about Marie Antoinette,

a film in which an ant saves itself from drowning
        in a glass of grape juice, crawling from the liquid

& stumbling, purple & wet, along the rim.
        A psychic skims C.'s palm & sees

he was stabbed through the back with a spear
        in a past life, most likely by his own soldiers.

Right before the guillotine dropped, Marie Antoinette
        apologized to her executioner for stepping on his shoe.

Eons of this. Tiredness. Cloudy beer. A bird,
        no, a plane, happening across the sky so slowly.

How artless, this one foot in front of the other,
        this waiting for the bruise to go blank.

Today, the sun did something invisible to the soil.
        Tomorrow, it will do it again.

The Decline and Fall of the Roman Empire

Shooing the committee of vultures, I garbage bag
the body of the raccoon & drop it off as a donation
at the gates of the wolf conservation center.

Zephyr, my favorite, hobbled by dewclaws
& white as eggshells, is kept in a separate pen
so he doesn't try to kill his sister again.

My mind is a liar. It wants you to live forever.
My language is flattened by this want. The pond
where Zephyr drinks, perfectly still, no threat

of spilling over, is overshadowed on all sides
by trees that speak to each other in words
unsullied by all these booming consonants,

these diphthongs the mouth conjures up
when it can find the courage to plead. For the trees,
leaf rot just means leaf rot. A wolf at the door

means a wolf at the door. Later, over pills
of dusted lion's mane mushroom, I will try
my best to give you, in the cleanest diction possible,

a series of facts to wrap yourself around.
The image of Zephyr, resisting the urge to bite, licking
the dirt caked deep in the scars on my knuckles.

The ghost of a rainbow in the frayed mist of a sprinkler.
The sliver of a daymoon reflected in a puddle
of liquid leaking from a backup generator.

In return, you will tell me of a woman whose tumor
outlived her for fifty years, growing even larger
under lab observation in Silicon Valley.

You will bask teary-eyed in the miracle
of simple truths, teaching me that a herd
of elephants is called a memory. We could make a life,

filling the room with words like these, saying nothing
that we mean. Wolf saliva heals wounds.
A group of feral cats is called a destruction.

The Decline and Fall of the Roman Empire

None of this body is what I began with.
I sacrificed a few brain cells for a sachet
of dollars. Paid for a flight to Rome

to witness the blessing of the throats,
the priest lifting the candelabra sculpted
in the shape of a vertebra to the necks

of the parishioners, scalding their skin
into perfect health. I wanted to live there,
but not in the ancient cobblestones

dragging history around by its tail, not
in the god-drunk frescoes lime-plastered
to their domes. No, I wanted

to live in the flame.

The Decline and Fall of the Roman Empire

Scratched into the canvas beneath a tumbling clot of red pigment,
a fragment of language, a stray missive from that bashful tent city

called heaven, the paint whispers *Like a fire that consumes all before it,*
& shy as gods, we listen, bracing ourselves for the tendrils of flames

we do our best to remind ourselves are just events, brief occurrences,
not objects we can hold in our hands like the tumors they will cut

from your lungs & send home with you as souvenirs in little pink vials
of formaldehyde, emblems of the body outracing the body at last,

the body you must now make peace with, saddling it up to leave
the museum & dive deep into the matter of time, central Philadelphia,

the words overlaying the sights *Like a fire that consumes all before it,*
the smokestacks of the oil refinery, the molting pigeons, the man tonguing

his golden delicious apple, the precambrian drone of jetliners, all points for
& against the argument that fire might have a purpose, like Emperor Nero

after the great flames fanned by summer winds left Rome in rubble,
how he used the smoldering debris to soak up the malaria-ridden marshes

that had plagued the city for generations, debris from the fire
it is rumored he started himself, a perfect circle, this tumbling clot

of our carrying on, *Like a fire that consumes all before it,* even itself, gaining
mass as it moves, not an object but an event, an event we've ignored

the invitation to, & still do, laughing in its face when you say
let's jump, but don't, for now, looking down from the bridge

at the Delaware River in the midst of October, the toxins of its oil-black
waters, the squelch of its tugboats, an open mouth that could consume

any fire that came before it, a triumph that you're still here to picture this:
the body, flame-licked & tattered, a matter of time, released

calmly into the ice-cold rapids, the end of a long sentence.

The Decline and Fall of the Roman Empire

Cutthroat trout. Advil fragments in the rose bed.
Peak radiation mutating the reproduction
of the goshawks that stalk my seed feeder.

To qualify for the experimental treatment,
you hope that your white blood cells stabilize,
that you *never stop listening to the songs of birds,*

cracking a joke, quoting the conservationist who,
seeking to capture with his paints the green
heron in stillness, strung wires through its wings.

If I want news of your progress, I hold my phone
above my head where the magpies flit through
the coursing waves of invisible signal.

I carry a raft of logs to the fireplace
to spend my minutes alongside
their burning, the embers glinting like amber

as they fizzle in & out of spacetime. Outside,
a deer lowers its long neck, losing its head
in the tall grass. Noting the quality

of the light through the window, I fail
to qualify it. There is nothing
left for you in nature.

A flight of shrews invades the mole hole.
Black aphids siphon the sap from the stem
of the mock orange until it curls.

II.

The Decline and Fall of the Roman Empire

At the heart of the palace
Nero built from the wreckage
of the great fire he started himself,
visitors can find a domed room
in the shape of an octagon,
where the emperor, through tricks
the light played on the walls
drowning in gold leaf,
manifested his divine will,
constructing an interactive ceiling
that rotated like the celestial rings
of the heavens, operated by his slaves
as his guests ate their lavish dinners,
spraying perfume, dropping
rose petals into their goblets
of wine in such insurmountable
quantities that the guests
were forced to swallow the flowers,
some vomiting the lumps of pink
matter back into their bowls, others
choking to death, smothered
in filth with smiles on their faces,
thankful for the bountiful gifts

of the loving god the emperor
burnt down the empire
to become.

The Decline and Fall of the Roman Empire

In his bone room, Thomas Jefferson
displayed the skulls & tusks

of woolly mammoths, polished
to a glisten with white vinegar.

Some men want the past to stay still.
Others would like it to arch its back.

My father, corralling the mess, keeps
the biographies of presidents on his bookshelf,

arranged by the color of their spines.
Days of Fire, American Phoenix, American Lion.

Having a form of dominion, he names
the source of every animal noise

echoing from beyond the dense tree line,
correcting my baseless assumptions.

What I thought was the snort of a ghost
is a deer with a broken hoof, stuck in a cattle grate.

What I thought was a screaming woman
is the agony of a red fox in heat.

One night, in anger, he towered over me,
pelting my torso with crumpled up dollar bills.

The nature of the punishment was unclear.
Something dog-like was barking.

When I flattened out the money,
the dead men stared, frozen in their green ovals.

The Decline and Fall of the Roman Empire

Mount Vernon

For thirty dollars, we can glimpse rooms
of battle swords, silk pouches of powdered wigs,

& a pair of the president's dentures
fashioned from the teeth of a dead horse.

Outside, the tourists force their noses
into the mouths of flowers to sniff

the history, snapping pictures
of the rows of yellow daffodils framing

the slave memorial, stuck in the lavish
shadows of giant white oaks.

J. & I walk through the trimmed grass,
talking fathers. Their love for bloodsport,

their fists of hairy knuckles, a pinkie ring
turned inward to sharpen a slap,

cruelties we can't find our way out of,
cruelties that pock each corner of this

leaf-blown landscape drowning
in another century's noise. Musket blasts

echo from hidden speakers. A rent-a-cop
twirls his nightstick by the gristmill

as the heavy wind churns into curds
of harsh weather. Wind that rips through

the colonnades, ruffling the witchy hair
of the spanish moss. Wind that tests

the pole's hold on the earth as it beats
the star-studded flag into knots.

The Decline and Fall of the Roman Empire

Today, I drank coffee in the shadow
        of the substation & placed a bet on the falcons.
The word ziggurat came to mind.
        The fake memoirs of Emperor Hadrian.

When the surgeon called your father's kidney
        a kidney, the kidney failed.
When I asked you to touch me,
        you zipped past *touch* to a place

where all language can do is crumble
        in the wake of its brutal task.
A windowpane. A face pushed into it.
        The awareness, like a ringing in the ear,

that the bluebells outside the room
        are only seldom blue, in a certain light.
Tonight, you said you picture God
        as a man because you miss your father.

Tonight, we shared a root beer float
        & promised we'd never have children,
while the Ford Explorer of clouds
        hovered above, threatening rain.

On the way home, I bought
    a family-sized pouch of Tide Pods,
a white noise machine
    that can mimic the sea.

The Decline and Fall of the Roman Empire

Rome, NY

As we pass through the rows of graves, some slanted
with age, others upright with the crisp texture
of the just-born, you fondle the CVS bag with the two tests
the box promises are bestowed with the faulty accuracy
of anything that can predict the future.
We inspect your tampon, saturated with rusty blood,
in a bathroom converted from the ruins of a mausoleum.
You insist the splotches are shaped like the heads
of German shepherds, yet when I look,
I only see the faces of stopped clocks.
Closer to the fluorescent light, maybe an evergreen tree.
We agree to disagree. Skipping half-relieved over the bones
of the man who penned the pledge of allegiance, you say
you would've named it after one of Jupiter's moons.

*

At Applebee's, we drink the champagne of beers,
while the old man at the bar describes how to quiet
the rattle of a gun rack with bifurcated baseballs.
He mentions the gout in his toe, *the disease of kings,*
how Agent Orange left him unable to bear a son.

I'm heirless, he laments, fumbling with his chicken irresist-a-bowl.
In the sweaty bathroom stall, we collate our bodies together
because we can, because we have these endless limbs
at our service, these time bombs in our chests.
Placing my pinky finger in your mouth, you threaten
to bite clean through it. We will stumble into the future like this.
Tallying the plastic bags as they drift by on the canal.
Counting the confederate flags at Ron's Bargain Barn as we learn
how to hack up a diseased tree into useful pieces of lumber.

The Decline and Fall of the Roman Empire

Rome, NY

In my favorite picture of you, the hair blown across
your face, obscuring your face, it's easy to make out,
deep in the distance, the hangers of the air force base
classified as a Superfund site, a sprawling huddle
of buildings expanding out into the extent of the valley.
Volatile organic compounds, the report says. *Solvents*
poured into the aquifer. Hair blown across your face,
obscuring your face, & beyond it, a tree, its leaves
wafting in a single direction, further evidence for the wind
that once carried into the rolling green hills the ash
& wreckage of the failed fighter jet tests run by
the bombardment wing. A wind, non-transferable into image,
except for its consequence. A face, erased, blotted out
by the hair that I would part, if the moment wasn't gone.
Out of sight, like the discarded munitions lining the three
identical landfills the picture lacks the dimensions to contain,
covered, as they are, by sheets of concrete, your face
no longer a face but an artifact hiding what's hidden.
The film-forming foam, the layers of lead-based fuels
that seeped for years into the water wells, now dormant,

frozen in time the moment I cracked open the aperture
of the lens, flooding it with color, overexposing the image
until everything in my sight was obscured by light.

The Decline and Fall of the Roman Empire

In the critically-acclaimed film, applauded
    for its portrayal of a world oversaturated

with image, we watch a boy watch a video
    of a pig being murdered with a bolt gun.

Earlier, a visit to the botanical gardens, the magnolias
    in full bloom, the circular nodules

at the center of the edging candytuft, the dangling
    carpets of the snow-in-summer bushes.

All the little devils are proud of hell.
    I wish I were a cannibal, you read to me

from *The Trouble with Being Born*
    forging a kind of love, rolling between

pools of sunlight to stay warm, *we should be excused*
    from lugging a body, you continue, as I spill a pebble

from my sneaker in order to test my heart, taxing it
    to shreds on the machine we've built to mimic a hill.

We swallow our elliptical pills. We ask Alexa to list
　　the bodily sensations of bone spurs.

We pass through the hours until they stiffen
　　into a slurry of smeared pixels.

A cop patrolling his sliver of grid, a pink rose
　　hanging from the pocket below his pepper spray.

A blood-red moon above the vein clinic.
　　A luminescent cocktail called *the yellow bird.*

The Decline and Fall of the Roman Empire

A man I often spend my time with,
in love with the accumulation of money,

shows me the spreadsheet where he hedges
his bets against the market & its assessment

of the world's materials. Close analysis is his work.
The sheer capacity. The volatile futures.

At the top of one column, the word *Diamonds*
in bold, next to its neighbor *Crude Oil,*

the crooked hillocks of its projected worth
bookmarked on his Robinhood app.

It is summer in October. He blasts
music filled with pangs of metallic noise.

At the edge of the pool shaped like a kidney,
the filter burbles with the bodies of frogs

swept by rain into the chlorinated water,
the jacuzzi designed to empty its excess

down a marble chute & into a granite grotto
where the water sits, collecting ecosystems

of bugs, huge bundles of leaves,
until someone he forgets the name of

comes & removes the mess with
a net attached to a bendable pole.

The world spills over with
its embarrassment of riches.

He asks me what, in the end,
I believe my words will be worth.

I think God is moving its tongue,
the singer screams, nearly blowing out

the bluetooth speaker tucked
behind the manicured bushes.

The Decline and Fall of the Roman Empire

State Fairgrounds

The story of
its ruin is simple
& obvious.

Between sips of beer,
the farmer speaks
with pleasure

of how expert
his mutant corn is
at killing caterpillars.

We watch two men
try to break
each other's arms

in a blow-up pool
filled with coleslaw,
grabbing at hocks

of flesh as they topple
over into golden pockets
of floodlight.

A veteran of two wars
fires a rocket launcher
at a clay pigeon.

A bumper sticker
promises *God*
is just around the corner.

Below the tilt-a-whirl,
a clown douses a sword
in lighter fluid,

strikes a match,
& shoves the blade
down his throat, flames first.

The Decline and Fall of the Roman Empire

There's a certain way empires grow, splintering
as they dilate, diffused with the invisible breath

of an imperial will that, if not voluntarily inhaled,
is forced upon each citizen to the furthest edge

of its limits, mouths gulping air like weary beaks swallowing
chunks of rodent crushed in procession

as war elephants stampede across treacherous
mountain ranges, the breath inside the lung inside

its trellised cage of bone huffing & puffing *who goes there*
to the land it devours in more than name alone,

the parasitic wasp bursting ready to mate from the torso
of a zombified cockroach, a cancer cell shucking

the slipshod shell of a vital organ while, on the TV,
the raiders intercept a fumble, a theme *we expand*

to its bulk, as Melville puts it in the chapters after
Tashtego climbs with a shovel into the severed

head of a sperm whale tied to the stern
    of the Pequod to source from the corpse

all the raw material he can muster, pushing himself
    further & further into the skull as he flenses

the blubber, tilling the borders he tunnels
    through, ramming a kind of ownership

down its throat until, in the span of a single breath,
    the rope snaps.

The Decline and Fall of the Roman Empire

The Mosquito Squad is fogging
        the neighbor's lawn with a yellow gas

the flyers warn can cause brain tumors
        with frequent exposure.

Inside, over coffee, my brother says
        he dreamt all morning he was a knight

hidden in a copse of trees
        before a raid on an enemy army,

& that after waking up, he knew
        with a kind of scary pride that the blood

spattered over every inch of his rusted
        chain mail armor wasn't his own.

Google tells him the dream means
        he's anxious for his calculus exam.

I see us in this room, like a city buried
        beneath the city of its conqueror.

We were younger, shaping our shouts into a form
        that only fists could puncture.

That was two & a half presidents ago.
        Someone we loved was dying slowly.

Now, we wait to crack open our several windows
        until we are told to.

Later, lathered in bug spray, we will go drink
        orange wine & listen to a nervous wreck

bastardize Vivaldi on his cello
        in the town amphitheater.

Without evidence, I assume there will be,
        at the very least, a few more years of this.

III.

The Decline and Fall of the Roman Empire

When a train derails, crumbling car by car
into a mess of metal & oil, an explosion occurs,
a sudden flexing of particles outward & into
the boundlessness of the American prairie
that generates so much heat physics simply refuses
to let it disappear, lingering on the horizon for days
as a plume, or as shroud, or as whatever word I decide
is the most accurate container for this immensity
tottering on the brink, this toxic mass I wish to describe
as *billowing* for the quality of its sound, how it brings
the tip of my tongue to my two frontmost teeth
in the effort of enunciation, in the effort of clarification,
getting down clearly & succinctly the invasion
of benzene into the groundwater, the proliferation
of raindrops that disperse into red rashes
when they meet the skin, a fact I can shape into
an image from a safe distance, for now, scrambling
the syntax, futzing with the font, spooling out
my sentence with the corpses of minnows & crayfish
until it collapses under its own weight, splintering
into shards that menace the entire landscape,
the words piling up on top of each other
until they congeal into a giant black cloud
it is impossible to see through.

The Decline and Fall of the Roman Empire

The day they ask if you'd rather
be burned or buried,

the president crashes
his bike into a sand dune.

Sitting in the long waiting room
between seconds, I notice you,

made god-like by your pain,
wrapping the world around your finger,

pushing the cursor forward & back,
pausing for glints of detail

in the periphery of the shaky video:
the spokes of the wheels drenched

in the reflection of the whitecaps
slapping the shore in the distance,

the surprised look of the man
collapsed on his side, useless

as a bouquet of lilies
sagging next to a hospital bed,

fallen before he ever had the chance
to learn he was falling.

It comforts you, how in a time
before all this history,

something brutal & long gone
like a sabertooth tiger

is slowly licking its cub
into a deep, peaceful sleep.

Down the hall in the children's ward,
we watch as a little boy draws

thick lines on a toy horse
with a sharpie, inventing the zebra.

The Decline and Fall of the Roman Empire

You grow convinced that God, who isn't real, is a woman, & that when she greets you, even though she won't, she will have six eyes & a tail & will kiss you, lipless, on the scar tissue ringing your chemo port.

The people who never happen are the most beautiful. Pure potential. The jelly sack of tadpole eggs we reached down from our pelican boat to puncture with a stick, killing softly what we meant to free.

Keats, in a letter to a man who outlived him: *I compare human life to a large Mansion of Many Apartments, two of which I can only describe, the doors of the rest being as yet shut upon me.*

I open the door. I drink a can of Liquid Death sparkling water. *At Verizon, my voice is my password,* I repeat for the robot on the other end of the phone, just so I know she knows I'm real.

Gibbon, describing the isolation of emperors: *the end comes only when we can no longer talk with ourselves.*

It is almost the end now. You reach out your living hand & I reach back.

Flying over Rome on Google Earth, I zoom into the piazza where Keats died, looking for a hard fact. I only see cars, hazy dots of matter, sinking into the cobblestones. A person, or a bush, holding a bloody cloth, or a rose.

The Decline and Fall of the Roman Empire

In the fabricated memoirs of Emperor Claudius, the emperor reads a fabricated poem in the voice of the oracle, predicting Rome's one-hundred-year enslavement to a procession of hairy men.

One will ride steeds with "toes for hooves." Another will gift Rome "poisons & blasphemies" & die from a "kick of his aged horse" that carried him as a child.

I read these words in a book in a library endowed by a man who performed unspeakable acts upon his grandchildren, a man who bought his wife a tiara encrusted with diamonds stolen from a deposed queen.

Outside the library, a park filled with jump-ropers, fountains, & benches modified to prevent the sleeping of exhausted bodies. I strut below the arch imitating an arch constructed to celebrate the deification of Emperor Titus. An arch peppered with sculpted facsimiles of the empire's pilfered objects—golden trumpets, fire pans, & menorahs—squished between the fluted columns.

Before I closed the book, Claudius, the copy, occupied by voices like a puppet, confessed to having "put the good of the Empire before all human consideration."

If I want to get home, I have to drive on a freeway named after a congressman, arriving at a fork in the road where, depending on whether an accident has occurred, I can either take a tunnel named after a governor or a bridge named after a president.

The Decline and Fall of the Roman Empire

Tate Modern

Inside the museum,
        a distraction from grief,

an Alpine ibex built from the broken
        legs of a wooden chair.

Outside the museum, a patch of roses,
        lab-conjured purples & oranges,

the overhead buzz
        of a drone designed

to vibrate like a cicada
        as it records.

It would very much like it
        if I made a scene.

*

Debt is the only spoken language.
        Men in pitch-black suits

whisper nearby, predicting the future
        volatility of the Japanese Yen.

They will stretch their lunch hour
        until it breaks,

stopping here & there to take
        each other's picture

with the Giacometti sculpture
        of a starving dog,

waving at the camera
        through the hole in its stomach.

*

In the Infinity Mirror Room, we find ourselves
        multiplied, sieved through with light,

pre-verbal & formless, slathered
        in a galaxy of microplastic stars.

God, inch by inch,
    is losing its purpose.

No noun could hold all of this endless space,
    but we will speak until we capture it.

In thirty minutes, the bankers will return
    to the trading floor & I will go bury a friend.

If you look closely, you can even see
    the future from here.

The Decline and Fall of the Roman Empire

Innovations in clock technology
can be traced back to the need
to carve out more time in the day for God.

I shake the little crystals in my wristwatch.
Aerosols dampen the afternoon sunlight,
confusing the roosters.

Receiving the news of the swollen abdomen,
the thinning out of the white blood cells,
I toss stalks of asparagus into the grass

& read the future based on how they land.
The field crowds around my addition to it.
For all I know, the squirrels are cursing at me.

Once, we fed ourselves computer duster,
weeks-old salami, & curdled milk. We invented nouns
for the wafts of pink exhaust that rise

like thought bubbles from the asphalt plant.
Our bodies happened to us so fast. The roosters
are screaming, believing it's already tomorrow.

The Decline and Fall of the Roman Empire

To accurately describe the cancerous body,
you resort to Freud: *the nature of horror*

is when the home becomes unhomelike.
The cowardly liver. The lionizing bedsores.

The people you love invested in
the particulars of a pain they can't see.

If the cancer could speak, you say
it would say: *I am calling from inside the house.*

The pain is the pain of creation. The pain
is the making of room for yourself inside yourself.

The Decline and Fall of the Roman Empire

Fox with Dead Rooster and Poultry
Melchior d'Hondecoeter
(1678, oil on canvas)

What drips from the fox's snout
is unmentionable. I don't have the words for it.

Inches from its paws, flightless birds
are painted into the eternal posture

of pointless effort: the flapping of useless wings,
beaks tilted up at a sky that always refuses.

I'm meant to adore these renderings
of the beautiful colors of their struggle.

The vibrant green paint of a mallard's head,
open-mouthed & bleating, synthesized

with verdigris & garden mulch, the yellow
of a lost empire's ruins in the distance

blended with the urine of a cow
fed exclusively on mango leaves.

I don't have the words for it,
the words that say *something has died here.*

They outrun description. They thicken
these depictions of faultless clouds.

In the gift shop, I find a print
of the painting rolled up

into a cylinder & crammed
in a cardboard tube.

The Decline and Fall of the Roman Empire

There are no images here, the professor says,
reading the poem in which I picture your death.

He leaves a question mark
next to a description of the thousands

of beats a hummingbird's heart fumbles
its way through each minute,

a dotted line of red ink struck-through
the epitaph found on a Roman gravestone:

I did not exist, I have existed,
I do not exist, I feel no desire.

You are nowhere to be found.
I've lassoed my language around

a copse of ash trees that was raised
only to be shaved down

into the smooth barrels of baseball bats,
& all I discovered was a run-on sentence.

I've hoisted my descriptors through
the thin chasms of Antelope Canyon

where the sandstone folds back on itself
like a frozen wave, an image

the professor believes I have to *dirty up,*
curling, with my words, the sandstone

inward like a slug, suffocating us
as we compress our diaphragms

to slide between the jutting fragments
of rock, an image that should stab

the reader in the eye, because somebody
was alive & now they aren't & we need to *feel it.*

I want you to describe this & only this,
the professor says, placing a bruised

empire apple on the desk,
leaving me alone in an office

filled with yellowed volumes
of slim, successful elegies.

Picturing his rows of perfect teeth,
I write down nothing of substance,

dreaming of limbs sprouting from the fruit's
ruby red skin, granting it a life it is already losing.

I wipe the sweat from the apple's forehead
& hum a lullaby into its ear.

I beg the apple to breathe.
I kiss the apple on the mouth.

The Decline and Fall of the Roman Empire

Trumpet, a bloodhound, won Best in Show
the day the chemo failed you.

Nonetheless, the world to put into words,
a turquoise marble in a toddler's mouth.

Nonetheless, turquoise, toddlers, fitful
patterns of weather in the sunniest winter

on record, the steam devils, the landspouts,
screengrabs of a photograph of the tree

of heaven spinning its windmills of
whirlybirds, deepfaked into phosphorescence,

a slice of nature I bring to you bedside,
scribbling elegies for the many things

I don't want you to miss, toggling
between black, red, or liver

to describe the folds of skin
sagging from Trumpet's chin.

I write down the words "fossil on a budget."
I write down an anaphora of tomorrows,

populating them with gluey moonlight & whale
sightings, the safety of the ocean from the shore.

Tomorrow, when the doctors say,
heads tilted towards their chests,

that there is nothing they can do,
I will write down each word carefully.

I will make nothing happen, forever.

The Decline and Fall of the Roman Empire

Orange Band, the last of its species,
the endling of the dusky seaside sparrows,
named after the metal tag clipped to its leg, died
in a cage on Disney World's Discovery Island.

I am told by your mother that when you left
your body, there was a sound. A warble.
The faint chirping of machines, she says.
Muffled singing behind a door.

IV.

The Decline and Fall of the Roman Empire

1.

The Physical Impossibility of Death
in the Mind of Someone Living
Damien Hirst, 1991
(Glass, painted steel, silicone,
monofilament, tiger shark,
formaldehyde solution)

To fabricate a perfect body,
the gallery peeled the skin

from the rotting shark, stretching it
over a fiberglass mold the artist

complained lacked the tonnage
of something pulsing with life.

Today, I stare the real thing straight
in the face. Two black dots for eyes.

A mouth I wish I could offer my head.
One tank over, there is a brown calf

petrified in formaldehyde, pierced
by a quiver of technicolor arrows.

On the wall, a stained-glass window
I can't see through, patched

haplessly together from a mesh
of splintered butterflies.

2.

For the Love of God
Damien Hirst, 2007
(Platinum, diamond, human teeth)

I rifle through the rooms looking for it.
The human skull the artist purchased

from a pawn shop, encrusting it in polyps
of pear-shaped diamond, pocking

its jaw with a fresh set of clean teeth,
seeking to wrangle a new shape from its death,

like the vial of poppyseeds I've kept
pocketed in lieu of your ashes, waiting

for the proper place to scatter them into potential.
I am told by an attendant that the skull

has been sold, that it now sits perched behind glass
in the office of a private investment firm.

Instead, she directs me towards another piece
she believes will capture my interest:

a piglet corpse the artist fused so firmly
to the wings of a dove, it turned into an angel.

3.

Mother and Child (Divided)
Damien Hirst, 1993
(Glass, stainless steel, perspex,
acrylic paint, cow, calf,
formaldehyde solution)

Two cows, sliced down the middle.
Two cows, cleaved into disparate parcels

of corpse one can saunter straight through, a tank
to either side of the walkway, a chance to gather

what the body can do only after it is done.
To parcel the animals into language requires

finding a better word for the color of blood.
To gather them into a corral of adjectives,

one must cattle-prod the herd into submission,
draining the heifers of their butterfat, practicing

a particular human cruelty on the beefcows,
forging beautiful names for each cut of their meat.

When I can ignore the screams of the visible,
the only word for the color of blood is blue.

When I try my best to describe you,
I barely make it past the skin.

4.

A Thousand Years
Damien Hirst, 1990
(Steel, glass, flies, maggots,
MDF, bug zapper, cow's head,
sugar, water)

Nothing here is lucky to be alive.
In one tank, hordes of flies are hatched

only to be dragged towards the stench
of rancid meat & the glossy light

of the insect-o-cutor, plummeting in little
dead bunches to the ground, as art.

On a table, sculptures of brick-sized pills.
In the corner, fat bowls of honeycomb

teeming with bees, the same shade as the orange flares
of poppy you will someday be. It is all big enough

to swallow us whole. These polka dots, this death-
stench, this shark jaw the artist has wrenched

apart as a reminder of the impossible thought
we can't stop thinking. This artist whose belly we are in.

This artist who believes there are no limits to what
can be achieved with a twisted mind & a chainsaw.

V.

The Decline and Fall of the Roman Empire

First, the muscles slacken,
flattening the slopes of the biceps

into valleys, jimmying open the jaw
for anything to crawl in or out with ease.

The eyelids flutter freely.
Flightless birds, we say to ourselves

in our inside voices. *Blueberries,*
we say, looking at the lifeless lips.

The liver, as it fails, spills over,
a twitching balloon collapsed

against a bed of sternum the skin
stresses the sculptural elegance of

as it tightens around the bone.
The kidneys whistle. The stomach honks.

It is a matter of fact. The lungs crash
hours before the heart, the fibers purpling

into plum-like portents of disaster,
clogging the airway with clots.

Hunched over like a gorilla,
a cell coughs up a cell.

The brain, shrouded in chemicals,
remembers a tongue, a carousel,

a few gravestones, the endless
salt flats choked with shadow.

The thinking is otherwise
unexceptional. The soul is yellow.

The Decline and Fall of the Roman Empire

The Son of Man
René Magritte
(1964, oil on canvas)

In the painting
all that is human
about the man

has been subsumed
by the apple
digested by it

lacking a glance
of the eyes there's no
way to suss out a threat

no way to mop up
the beauty I have
come to collect

& be transformed by
behind him a barren sky
another blank

blue mind hemmed in
by the false comfort
of clouds

emptied of blood
our faces sink down
inside themselves

lose all specificity
the featureless death
masks of pharaohs

buried alongside
locks of hair
& golden diadems

the headless wooden
figurines of their slaves
sculpted from wax

how can I
lift your face
from your face

with what can I
silence this mouth
foaming with nouns

I will refuse my breath
until I am as lungless
as a blowfish

I will eat clumps
of paper until
I turn into a tree

The Decline and Fall of the Roman Empire

After the funeral, I trudged through bursts
of sewage, passed the shit-roosting monarchs,
dodged the assaults of the noon bats, & shattered
my knuckles against the bark of a catalpa.

Someone I loved was an urn of dust
stacked on top of a copy of *The Power Broker.*
I was a man made of acute angles.
I let anything touch me in my crooked places.

Hand plastered in a cast, I went on & on
about toothy pain & necktie nooses,
until Dr. So & So passed me a pamphlet
watermarked with little Jesuses.

I gorilla-glued a life together.
I called my senator. I funneled worms
of yellow powder up through a dollar
& into my nostril. I fed my pain

a cheeseburger & cleaned its clammy teeth.
Sometimes, I was just a bag of meat
standing too close to the lip of a bridge
in the depression between two hills.

Sometimes, the sun sat low in the sky,
& if I stared at it with closed eyes, I could
watch fruit loop after fruit loop of thought
coalesce into the confused faces of my dead.

All this wonder made me wince.
Bones fusing back into a fist, white bread
slathered in suds of grape jelly,
the rainbow trout thumping up a fish ladder

in the video I watched while I practiced
my crappy slip knots. Blurred scraps
of color in the distance, I thought they could
teach me what to do with my hands.

I was patient. The fact of their bodies
was buried in the fact of the water.
Each second happened a second
after a second until the video stopped.

The Decline and Fall of the Roman Empire

To experience what some call *animal joy*
Requires latching your sorrows
To a goat & sending it wandering

Through rolling hills of pachysandra
Requires lifting the speaker of a cell phone
To the gusty winds so Song Sleuth can identify

The melodious names of the birds
By their trills *bobolink cowbird oystercatcher*
In a lecture I learned that one can discern

The strength of an empire by its belief
In the self-sovereignty of its wild creatures
Emperor Commodus slaughtering a hundred lions

In a single day to a packed crowd in the colosseum
A crocodile the size of car locked in a cage
In the middle of a Florida steakhouse

It's true I've mistaken myself for the master of
These manifold acorn worms
These numerous chicken turtles

Once I believed I even caught a glimpse
Of your ghost in the opal eyes of a rottweiler
Carrying a stick around the rim

Of a pond littered with swan boats
Just a trick of light bouncing off
The mirrored wings of the metal animals

Just another failure in the effort to
Anthropomorphize the rain
Lending it your voice & contours

Like some kind of reverse dictionary
I became the many pages
Of words between *loss* & *god*

Like some kind of derelict philosopher
Reckless with my language I gave
A name to my pain & called it *dog*

The Decline and Fall of the Roman Empire

It is a devilish kind of necromancy, my belief
in the supremacy of the dead & their refusal to quit

staying, their carrying on in the manner of clouds
the canonical poets exalt in their end-stopped elegies.

One, having lost a mentor, might observe "the blousy
front of cotton balls hopping across the alps."

Another, sick with consumption, might describe
the stratocumulus as "pure & white as flocks

new shorn" & we are forced to picture him as a sheep,
ready for god, a clean soul grasped in his outstretched hand.

In moments of peril, people, being people, look up,
praying for a swift end to their punishment,

hoping for a mirror, the contours of the human face
reflected back as fluffy clumps of weather.

"A sack of idle water." "A swollen fistful of mist."
On the day you died, there wasn't a single cloud in the sky.

The Decline and Fall of the Roman Empire

Inside the aviary, none
of the birds will look at me.

The blue-bellied rollers
hide their beaks

beneath their wings,
leaving little for a predator

to tear away, masking
the bare branches

as pedestals for
headless kernels of opal,

the wind's invisible syllables
stirring them into a frenzy.

They must smell my stink of several
unaccountable foreign objects.

Lime, sweat, & patchouli,
the inner walls of an incensed temple.

The crowned cranes let loose
their foghorns when I approach,

signifying their distaste,
contorting their lengths

into the zigzag omens
of bad health, the sound

sending the red-tailed hawk hurtling
headlong into the walls of its cage.

Change, the birds seem to say,
regarding my little life.

In one enclosure, a mother hocks up
a wriggling worm for its cohort of chicks.

Next door, in the effort for
"environmental enrichment,"

one of the conservationists
rips apart an intricate nest

of torn up phonebooks,
so that tomorrow, fresh mess

lining the humdrum habitat,
the southern ground hornbill

can put it back together again.

The Decline and Fall of the Roman Empire

The word of the day is *chasm*.

They are few & far apart, the hours.

In the mall, cars for sale: a guppy, a carisma.

Indebted to the state, I stir-fry the fiddleheads.

An egg yolk. A brainstorm. Sixty Novembers, or so.

The sun nodding off against the roof of the condo complex.

I wish to defer the inevitable. I lack the language for it.

Augenblick. A split second. A very short moment.

Tomorrow, the world will be what exactly.

Noise & its toddlers. Picnics in Wichita.

A grassy skull punctuated with laughter.

Something I have everything to do with.

Parasitic wasps, the removal of mountaintops.

Ambient pain in my ankle, I stir-fry the pork shoulder.

The word of the day is *pulverize*.

The word of the day is *bleat*.

I put a coin in the meter. I eat the meat.

The Decline and Fall of the Roman Empire

After your death, I google the mourning
practices of long gone bipeds, thinking
there are lessons to learn from bone,
thinking I could love the world,
if only I knew the world. (I find caves
covered in red ocher handprints.
Canopic jars of intestine & gold.)

*

The doctor diagnoses it as *ecological grief,*
the tears I shed over the extinction
of the mountain mist frog (invasive fungus,
habitat loss) & I suddenly feel like a wasp
ambushed by a cup. On the drive home,
I count the glowing eyes of the raccoons
living inside the abandoned Pizza Hut.

*

Life fitness. Ghost pepper. I think
I get the gist. We are inside our bodies
like bears in a blizzard. We are inside
these nostrils, these ribcages, propped

up by these faulty spinal cords,
forever living in a fourth-floor rental
at the intersection of Reservoir & Grape.

*

Some Neanderthals were buried
on beds of kaleidoscopic flowers.
The most stunning conflagration
of colors I've ever seen was the whirling
pinwheels of rainbow on the surface
of the Gowanus Canal. It shocks me,
the glamor I'll ascribe to any ruined thing.

*

The doctor says he wonders if the world
wished it saw us coming. (We think highly
of them, these abstract thoughts let loose
from the mind.) Tomorrow, I will go look
at twenty paintings of a single door.
I hope they will rivet me. I hope tomorrow
will be the tomorrow to end all tomorrows.

*

Today, the geese are flickering on & off
across the sky. The planet occurs to me
like an idea. Sure, I've heard grief
compared to the sea, a panther,
the tundra, but never likened
to this kind of weather. (Thirty-second
sun-shower. Daymoon that just won't let go.)

*

Here's what I know about the world.
When my sister lifts her boots from
the stirrups & spurs the soft hide
of her horse, the horse, startled
& surprised, trots faster, picking up
its pace, trying to outrun what is still
clinging to its back.

The Decline and Fall of the Roman Empire

There was always something—*goose, snow, bomb*—

falling in factions from the patchwork sky.

Feelings of grief were shared in the healing circle.

We lost sixteen species of tanager,

a deckle-edged copy of *Measure for Measure.*

Riding our gondolas to the aneurysmal altitudes

of ice-mantled cliffsides, tracking

the growth of our terrariums

squirming with blister beetles, we smelled

our funny smells & drank our banana slushies

half-laughing, half-crying, as the casket lift

lowered the last of our caskets into the earth.

We didn't know how much we would miss us.

To soothe us, the mannequin we called mother

bought us a stuffed baby mammoth.

The Decline and Fall of the Roman Empire

It's true, I will most likely die
in starchy sheets completely foreign

to me, but what am I to do,
for now, with this onion-light

reaching through the crosshatch
of conifer & hornbeam

I only notice because I wish
to be ordained with the truth,

absolutely smothered in it,
like the student who came to me

crying because he crushed
a cluster of ladybugs in anger.

In the hospital, you seemed to grow
closer to it—something silent

& translucent, a flinch of gossamer
soaked in names like the trophy case

of fishhooks dangling from
the mouth of a spotted bass.

We filled your ears with singing
as this emperor of bees, this potentate

of geysers, grabbed the steering wheel
& racked it all the way to the left.

I think I'm beginning to understand loss
as the loss of understanding.

The hornbeam is actually a serviceberry.
A group of ladybugs is called a loveliness,

my student teaches me, as I continue
correcting his mistaken remainders,

as I demonstrate this long division.

VI.

The Decline and Fall of the Roman Empire

On the cover of the children's book *Oil Spill!*,
a beaver shivers in a slick of chemicals
rendered in the flashy hues of a rainbow.

To test my student's knowledge of sight words,
the miasmic syllables of diagraphs, I have them repeat
the words back at me as I read: *boom, sticky, accident,*

hitching the descriptions to their images: a series of
animals pursued by giant billows of sludge morphed by
the illustrator into the ominous shapes of claws

& pincers, the clownfish swimming just out of reach,
blissfully at peace, the manatees diving to deeper layers
of sea, away from our vantage point on the disaster.

My students are six. They sip cups of pink lemonade
the color of dyed salmon. They will never die.
When I arrive at the drawing of a man in a hazmat suit

holding a seagull caked in pitch-black crude
out towards the reader, they crawl closer, reaching
their little hands up, trying to pet the paper.

The Decline and Fall of the Roman Empire

Eventually, people grew out of people.
People crying into their porchetta.
People thinking their complexities
into mush. People performing kind acts
in bad faith, relaxing into the shade
of their gazebos, admiring their views
of the new phenomena of nature,
rising heat levels basting the sky
into whip-fast funnels. Silly gooses, people.
Numbskulls. People tunneling into walls
of people sidetracked by swatches of language,
hating people, loving the hating of people,
mulling over the progress of the garden,
the proliferation of color, the spilling up
& over of stinky bushes they forget the names of.
Their memory fails them, people.
They're only human, people.
People peopling the valleyside into
the flurry of commerce, selling trinkets
& baubles, pretty lithographs of atrocities,
paper facsimiles of purple roses.
People weaving their planes through
chemtrails, skimming along the ozone, speeding
past a hawk tangled in a balloon string.

Queasy people, invertebrate & gorgeous
in the evening light. Klutzy people,
glossing over the tomfoolery of an oil spill.
Willy-nilly people, mumpish, pregnant
with joy, fumbling with the keypads & levers,
lowering the car window for a few fingers
of breeze, admiring the eruptions of mountains
surrounding the speedway, in awe of their own
transience, their brief blips of existence, snapping
their pictures of the floodplains,
the twirling blue pansies, the industry of beavers,
the isthmus of feldspar & freeze-thaw
that was here long before people
found people to steal it from.

The Decline and Fall of the Roman Empire

Chocolate cosmos or bittersweet shimmer.
Atomic tangerine or tiger's eye to describe

the color of the inferno toppling the tree line,
combusting the bark into clouds of particulate dust

the fire engines painted fire-engine red
disperse with their hoses of foam,

tinting the flames into a shade redolent
of baby carrots or tangerine peels, the safety

orange of traffic cones designed
to offset the azure of a healthy sky,

the opposite of this swath of crimson overhanging
the skyscrapers, this unbreathable sheen

one could compare to the many known gradations
of rose, such as brilliant, razzle dazzle, or folly.

When I open my mouth to it, I feel my liver shrivel.
An epoch teetering. Blood slithering, hunkered down,

through its vessels, more barn red than blood red,
less incarnadine & more vermillion, a pigment

the Roman painters utilized as a backdrop
to their portrayals of triumph, Priapus,

the god of fertility, weighing his cock against a bag
of coins on a set of scales, the winged goddess

of victory emerging, battle-worn, from a slurry
of imperial sky, a pigment synthesized by boiling

mercury in a flask until it vaporizes, condensing
as a toxic red ash that plasters the lungs

when inhaled, forming a color that, in order
to be seen, requires shattering the flask that holds it.

The Decline and Fall of the Roman Empire

Tallahassee, FL

In the twenty-minute ride to the airport,
Mark, my taxi driver, describes the unfurling
progress of his confederate jasmine,
how its spindly white flowers have colonized
the splintered stakes of his picket fence,
picking up the pace of its growth
as it sensed the space cleared to meet
the sprawl of its capacity, spraying
toxic sap as he tried to prune it back,
slicing the sunlight into wafers of shadow
beneath the uniform squares of the pergola
it has conquered. In my carry-on bag
is a book about pain. Its unsharability,
its resistance to language, its histories
stored in the darkest hiding places of the body
that spread & spread until they consume the body.
Outside the window, I see sixteen crucifixes
& a lizard carrying another lizard in its mouth.
A father dragging his toddlers down the sidewalk
by a leash. None of this suffering is original.
Because there is no winter here, Mark says
his plants will live forever.

The Decline and Fall of the Roman Empire

We knew what we'd become, so we became it

fast. It became us, this becoming,

this coming out from the caves & into canyons

the land cleared for us sensing what would

become of us, our sudden confluence of chromosomes,

our random combinations of disparate particles.

It came from nowhere, this comely planet,

the conifers, the common grackles,

the proof of our breath in the cold air,

our poisonous exhales of carbon.

We were becoming frightfully quick, with so much

force, that the force became our knowledge

& we became what we knew. Conundrums.

Cannoneers. A congregation of jackals.

It became us, knowing. It became

concerning, the chaos in the colonies,

the chloride in the aqueduct, the atrophy

in the congress, the crying of the children.

We were becoming better. Skyscrapers.

Puddlejumpers. Hundreds of definitions

for the word *run*. Soon, we would

become the best we'd ever been & save us

from what we had become.

The Decline and Fall of the Roman Empire

Salt Lake City, UT

Bring me the sunset
in a cup, my teabag says,
quoting Dickinson,
& how could I not
oblige, with this
smudge of goldenrod
sitting on the horizon
tinged with the fleshy
translucence of
a mangosteen,
this gaseous ball
of flames sinking
down below the snow-
capped mountains
I've already captured
thirteen identical photos
of, knowing very well
what grants the colors
the interstellar sheen
of a nebula—

the burping
exhaust of diesel trucks,
the huff of noxious dust
drifting off the rim
of the Great Salt Lake,
the clouds billowing up
into the atmosphere,
& caking against it
as so much dirt, smearing
into the appearance
of beauty, making
a kind of art, like Dickinson,
of their confinement
as chemicals in a world
of chemicals, as mindless
gauze blanketing
this miasma of
a night sky that
continues on & on
as I continue to end.

The Decline and Fall of the Roman Empire

I blinked & nearly
missed it completely.

A skirmish under the overpass.
A film by Michelangelo Antonioni.

Green soda spilled from the window
of a yellow taxi.

Fire turned a forest into fire.
Mushrooms & duck fat congealed in a pan.

Toddlers talked back & forth
between two soup cans & a shoestring.

Rain bounced off the skylight.
God was a cracker we ate.

When it outraced a missile,
a falcon was tossed

a frozen gerbil yanked
from a denim sack.

The Elk River gave us cancer.
Gum got stuck in the basil plant.

How else to describe it. We had underbites.
We wore big, black coats.

Somewhere along the way
the word for a little mouse

became the word for muscle
& I could finally carry

the air conditioner up the stairs.

The Decline and Fall of the Roman Empire

We are pushing up against

Something denser than air

The yoga instructor

Intones to her GoPro

As I contort my bones into

The Half Lord of the Fishes

Stretching the limits of

Muscles brimming with atoms

Fuzzy clouds of electrons

Jumbles of dots connected

By lines of terrible feeling

To other jumbles of dots

In bodies running low on time

We fold into baffling shapes

The One-Legged King Pigeon

The Happy Baby

Tunneling further inward

Breathing away the hours

Systems of stars born as

Collapsing balls of gas

That spin faster & faster

As they shrink

The Decline and Fall of the Roman Empire

Swarming with flea-sized ecstasies, pinpricked

with the scientific names of the numinous

bats that riot through the plum-dawn light,

I've lugged this hindbrain through funerals,

mitzvahs, & algebra, reciting *firecat,* reciting *cloud-puffball,*

subsisting on little more than speech-balloons & rain,

only to arrive at another streambed scintillating

with foamy prisms of toxic coal-cleaner still abounding

in bees, sticky-legged & busy, ceaselessly crawling

with damselflies in the midst of making more damselflies

thinking nothing of me caught up in my thinking

that the world is only what it is & I am on it,

I am in it like a turtle hitching a ride on the back

of an alligator to get from shore to shore.

The Decline and Fall of the Roman Empire

Like the two brains of a cuttlefish
conspiring to mimic a rock, I can
remake you into anything here.

An itchy soul. A conch shell.
A sack of yesterdays I drag past
the border of the retention pond,

the bald dome of the nuclear reactor
cresting above the tufts of flowers
trellised along its roadblocks—

a radiated head robbed of its hair.
I can make you the cuttlebone
filling the cuttlefish with air.

A barn freed of its burdensome owl.
A sexless snowglobe. A dogwood
diapered in dog flies. A dead sun.

I could fold & fashion
your hospice skin into
a lumpy cloud, reassemble

your left nipple as a survivor pea,
a navel orange, a socrates cucumber,
something I could easily crimp

my wordy tongue around,
saying & saying sentences
that point to where it hurts,

fibbing & fibbing until
I birth you, bloody & damp,
back into existence.

You are five hundred years old.
Your mother is a rhinoceros.
You chirp like a firebug.

In one hand, you are holding
a clutch of atoms, & in the other,
this tulip I've built for you.

Notes

The title of this collection is borrowed from Edward Gibbon's six-volume work *The History of the Decline and Fall of the Roman Empire.*

The epigraph is drawn from the poem "The Lord and the General Din of the World" by Jane Mead.

In "The Decline and Fall of the Roman Empire (The pianist rubs the misery)," the painting mentioned in the final lines of the poem is by Agnes Martin.

"The Decline and Fall of the Roman Empire (Scratched into the canvas beneath a tumbling clot…)" is after Cy Twombly's painting "Fifty Days at Iliam: The Fire that Consumes All before It."

"The Decline and Fall of the Roman Empire (In my favorite picture of you, the hair blown across)" is indebted to the poem "Sancho Panza" by Austin Araujo.

In "The Decline and Fall of the Roman Empire (In the critically acclaimed film, applauded)," the film mentioned is *Benny's Video* (1992) written and directed by Michael Haneke. The line "all the little devils are proud of hell" is an excerpted line of a dialogue from the film *Wake in Fright* (1971) written by Evan Jones and directed by Ted Kotcheff. *The Trouble with Being Born* is by Emil Cioran.

In "The Decline and Fall of the Roman Empire (A man I sometimes spend my time with)," the quoted lyrics at the end of the poem are lifted from the song "My Own Summer (Shove It)" by Deftones.

In "The Decline and Fall of the Roman Empire (Trumpet, a bloodhound, won Best in Show)," the final line is an adaptation of the line "poetry makes nothing happen" from the poem "In Memory of W.B. Yeats" by W.H. Auden.

In "The Decline and Fall of the Roman Empire (To fabricate a perfect body)," the final lines of the poem are an adaptation of a direct quote from Damien Hirst spoken upon his acceptance of the 1995 Turner Prize for "Mother and Child, Divided."

"The Decline and Fall of the Roman Empire (After your death, I google the mourning)" is indebted to Paul Otremba.

In "The Decline and Fall of the Roman Empire (To experience what some call *animal joy*)," the lines "I gave / A name to my pain & called it *dog*" are a quote from *The Gay Science* by Friedrich Nietzsche.

The book mentioned in "The Decline and Fall of the Roman Empire (In the twenty minute ride to the airport)" is *The Body in Pain* by Elaine Scarry. The word "unsharability" is borrowed from Scarry.

In "The Decline and Fall of the Roman Empire (Swarming with flea-sized ecstasies)," the phrases "firecat" and "cloud-puffball" are drawn respectively from the poems "Earthy Anecdotes" by Wallace Stevens and "That Nature is a Heraclitean Fire and of the comfort of the Resurrection" by Gerard Manley Hopkins. The line "the world is only what it is" is an excerpted line of dialogue from the film *Possession* (1981) written by Frederic Tuten and Andrzej Żuławski. The final lines of the poem are indebted to "Crescent" by C.D. Wright.

Acknowledgments

Thank you to the following publications in which these poems appeared previously, sometimes in different forms or with different titles:

32 Poems, The Adroit Journal, Afternoon Visitor, AGNI, American Literary Review, American Poetry Review, Blackbird, Cherry Tree, The Cincinnati Review, The Common, Copper Nickel, Denver Quarterly, Frontier Poetry, The Journal, The Los Angeles Review, Mississippi Review, The Missouri Review, The Nation, Ninth Letter, North American Review, Palette Poetry, Poet Lore, Poetry Online, Quarterly West, Redivider, Sixth Finch, Southern Indiana Review, Southeast Review, The Spectacle, Third Coast, Waxwing, West Branch, Yalobusha Review

"The Decline and Fall of the Roman Empire (Near the end of his life, the artist painted six coffins)" was reprinted in *Poetry Daily* and *Best New Poets* 2023.

My deepest gratitude to Four Way Books, Martha Rhodes, and Ryan Murphy for seeing something in these poems. And to Hannah Matheson, my editor, for championing me and for giving my work such unbridled attention. I owe this book to you.

Thank you to the creative writing programs at New York University and University of Utah for the support while I completed this book. And thank you to my teachers for helping me find my way to these poems: Michael Dumanis, Mark Wunderlich, Phillip B. Williams, Anna Maria

Hong, Annie DeWitt, Deborah Landau, Matthew Rohrer, Claudia Rankine, Ken Chen, Emily Skillings, and Rachel Zucker.

Thank you to Terrance Hayes for pushing me to find the ecstasy in my grief.

Thank you to Catherine Barnett for giving me the time, space, and consultation I needed to complete the earliest iteration of these poems. I will always be grateful.

Thank you to Timothy Donnelly for your generosity and inspiration.

And lastly, thank you to my peers, readers, family, and loved ones, especially Arianne Goodell, Lucas Jorgensen, Peter LaBerge, Luci Arbus-Scandiffio, Nicholas Pierce, Peter Voskuil, and Cormac Roth. You are in every word.

About the Author

Matthew Tuckner received his MFA in Creative Writing at NYU and is currently a PhD student in English/Creative Writing at University of Utah. His chapbook, *Extinction Studies*, is the winner of the 2023 Sixth Finch Chapbook Prize. His poems have appeared or are forthcoming in *AGNI*, *American Poetry Review*, *Kenyon Review*, *The Nation*, *The Adroit Journal*, and *Best New Poets*, among others.

We are also grateful to those individuals who participated in our Build a Book Program. They are:

Anonymous (5), Robert Abrams, Debra Allbery, Maggie Anderson, Jean Ball, Sally Ball, Adria Bernardi, Richard Blanchard, Laurel Blossom, Lee Briccetti, Anne Babson Carter, Jennifer Christman, Aaron Coleman, Peter Coyote, Elinor Cramer, Michael Anna de Armas, Brian Komei Dempster, Patrick Donnelly, Lynn Emanuel, Joan Frank, Rigoberto Gonzalez, Elizabeth T. Gray Jr., David and Joan Grubin, Naomi Guttman and Jonathan Mead, Beth Harrison, Jeffrey Harrison, KT Herr, Carlie Hoffman, Elizabeth Jackson, Linda Susan Jackson, Marilyn Johnson, Deborah Jonas-Walsh, Maeve Kinkead, David Lee and Jamila Trindle, Rodney Terich Leonard, Jen Levitt, Howard Levy, Owen Lewis and Susan Ennis, Ralph and Mary Ann Lowen, Maja Lukic, Ricardo Alberto Maldonado, Cleopatra Mathis, Victoria McCoy, Lupe Mendez, Mary Jane Nealon, Nicole Nevadunsky, Kimberly Nunes, Cathy McArthur Palermo, Veronica Patterson, Eileen Pollack, Martha Rhodes, Soraya Shalforoosh, Sarah Stone, Yerra Sugarman, Marjorie and Lew Tesser, Reed Turchi, Maria Walsh, and Calvin Wei